About the Author:

Mr. Aman Yadav works as an Assistant Professor at St. John College of Engineering and Management, Palghar, accredited to the University of Mumbai. Along with a few years of experience in teaching subjects like English, Communication Skills, Business Communication, Professional Communication and Ethics, and more, Mr. Aman Yadav is also a PhD scholar at Amity University Gwalior, Madhya Pradesh.

2015 saw the author graduate with a B.A. in English from K J Somaiya College of Arts & Commerce, Mumbai. From the University of Mumbai, Kalina, he earned his M.A. (Hons.) in English in 2017.

He also passed the UGC-NET exam in English subject, which was administered in March 2018.

Acknowledgements

I'm overjoyed to publish my debut book, titled "Acing Employment Skills." I have no doubt that it will significantly advance students' understanding and help them receive better training for locating suitable employment across various fields. The book covers some of the most crucial skills that students should acquire while in college or even after receiving their degrees.

I'd want to use this chance to express my appreciation for and recognise the efforts and contributions of a select group of people among many more. I want to start by expressing my gratitude to my entire family for their unwavering support and faith in me. I want to express my gratitude to my parents, older sisters, and brothers-in-law for their unending support and affection.

I also thank Prof. Dr. Iti Roychoudhury and Dr. Zeba Siddique, my PhD guide and co-guide, respectively, for their guidance and motivation in all my endeavors.

I also wish to use this platform to acknowledge and thank my dearest colleagues and friends, Dr. Eknath Patil and Mr. Elloit Cardozo for their invaluable support, advice, and instructions at every step of the way.

And lastly, I thank all my dear professors, friends, and colleagues who have always supported me through thick and thin and contributed to this book in one way or another.

I also specially mention and thank Mr.Aditya Sharma for beautifully designing the cover page of the book.

-Author

Table of Content:

Introduction

Employment skills are the fundamental knowledge, character traits, and morals that enable you to succeed in any workplace. These are also called 'enterprise skills', 'employability skills', 'communication skills' or 'workplace skills'.

Employment skills include things like:

- Communication skills
- Leadership
- Problem solving
- Teamwork
- Reliability
- Self-management
- Planning and organisation
- Initiative
- Learning

Communication Skills

It is a soft skill that is highly valued for all jobs and one of the most significant personality traits. It is easier to convey a message clearly when the five components of communication—the sender, receiver, message, medium, and feedback—are used effectively. A worker with effective communication skills helps the business avoid pointless misunderstandings and time wastage, which in turn boosts productivity.

Skills in verbal, nonverbal, visual, and written communication are all possible. You must be able to comprehend your coworkers' ideas and directives in order to communicate effectively at work. Additionally, you must persuade your coworkers of your thoughts and ideas in order to achieve your goals. With practise, communication becomes better. Keep a positive attitude, pay attention to other people, and think before you speak. Participating in clubs or on social media can both help you improve your communication skills.

Leadership

Every stage of an organisation requires strong leadership. Employers search for applicants with this skill set. If you can effectively manage your team members, inspire and train the staff to improve their work practises, and set objectives or goals for the coworkers to share in the interest of the company, you can demonstrate your leadership skills.

Problem solving

Determining the issue, locating the source of the problem, choosing the best course of action, and putting it into practise are all parts of problem solving. By resolving complex problems, a good problem solver aids in overcoming challenges. They are beneficial to any organisation because they increase the team's productivity.

You will need to conduct research, analyse the situation, and then decide on more complicated issues. You can divide a problem into smaller components before tackling the whole thing. Participating in brainstorming sessions, completing projects and research assignments, and even solving puzzles can all help to advance problem-solving abilities.

Some of the steps of problem solving are:

- Describe or identify the problem.
- Collecting data
- Recognize the interests or points of view of everyone
- List potential choices, then evaluate them.
- Select an option.
- Put a fix into action

Teamwork

The ability to understand your place within the team and get along with your teammates is referred to as teamwork. Teams must work together more than ever to increase productivity in the face of fierce global competition. Workflow improvements, improved coworker relationships, and higher job satisfaction all help teams perform better.

Collaboration is a necessary component of all jobs occasionally. A better workplace is a result of collaboration as a teamwork skill. Your chances of being hired by a company to assist in more effectively achieving the organization's goals are also increased. The stability, innovation, and productivity of the organisation are directly impacted by how well teams of employees work together.

Teamwork skills can be boosted by using the following:

- Recognize your individual team goal and comprehend your role's responsibilities.
- Utilize your time wisely and be clear about any deadlines, guidelines, or tasks' goals.
- Tell your coworkers how passionate you are about a project.
- Give your team members the respect and recognition they deserve.
- To resolve any conflicts, work effectively as a team.
- For more motivation and a positive outlook, join a sports team or take up a sport.
- Become a volunteer for organisations and lend a hand to coworkers at work to improve your teamwork abilities.

Reliability

Being trustworthy and dependable is a crucial employability skill because it promotes trust with the employer. The secret to reliability is consistency. Always stick to your schedule and deliver high-quality work. When you perform well at work and meet or exceed expectations, your reliability will increase. Make a daily to-do list and reply to inquiries right away. If there are mistakes, acknowledge them and learn from them so you can take deliberate steps to avoid repeating them in the future. Quality work implies minimal errors.

Self-management

The ability to plan and manage your work commitments consistently with little to no supervision and guidance is known as "self-management." This ability also promotes efficiency by saving time.

Self-management skills can be developed by:

- Assuming responsibility and requesting more responsibility at work.
- Being responsible for your actions and work.
- Managing your commitments and taking part in volunteer work.

Planning and Organisation

By effectively managing time, money, and effort, you can assist your employer in achieving their objectives. Being organised means being able to schedule your time and complete your work accordingly. You are aware of the task's importance, completion time, and required tools. Being organised involves using your creativity, acting on your own initiative, and making decisions.

Tips to develop your organisation skills:

- Make a schedule.
- Set objectives and action items.
- Plan your work.
- Set priorities for your work and create a schedule.
- Plan or coordinate activities that advance this skill set.

Initiative

Employers view initiative as a critical component of employability. Initiative is the drive to take preventative action and adjust to changing circumstances. You must first independently identify the opportunities and the client requirements in order to show initiative. Create strategic plans in accordance with the task or organization's goals in order to put the ideas into practise. People who are proactive are driven to succeed. They would constantly work to advance their knowledge and skills in an effort to better themselves. Such employees are valued by organisations and employers.

Initiative can be improved by:

- Contacting businesses and organisations to inquire about new opportunities
- Determining a plan's viability before putting ideas and solutions into motion
- Recommending policy changes while respecting cultural and political sensibilities

- Establishing neighbourhood charities or organisations

Learning

Employees who acquire new skills can increase their understanding of the company. Good learners typically adapt to change more quickly by picking up new ideas and techniques. They are useful to the company because they can expeditiously fill demanding positions and save time. A skills-based course, research, or picking up a new hobby can all help you advance your learning. The acquisition of skills guarantees a seamless transition to the use of new systems, processes, and technology. Employability skills continue to be essential for success given the fierce competition in the workplace.

Employers test all these skills in prospective employees. They look for people who can demonstrate sound judgment, good decision-making, and excellent communication abilities. Therefore, they use a variety of techniques and rounds as part of their selection procedures to assess these skills in the candidates in an effort to determine which individuals would be the best fit for their organization. Group discussion, personal interview, aptitude test, etc. are some of the common rounds of the selection procedure used by most of the recruiters. Hence, there's a need to equip oneself with the appropriate skills and knowledge required for cracking these rounds. By preparing well in advance, candidates can confidently face recruiters and convince them of their abilities.

Let's discuss these crucial rounds in much detail so as to make sure that we ace each of them and secure the desired job.

Group Discussion

Group Discussion is now a required step in the application process for high-paying jobs and admission to elite universities. Group discussions (GDs) now receive the same weight in the evaluation process as written tests and interviews for admission to business schools. Group discussions are frequently used in multinational corporations to evaluate some of the most important personality traits relevant to their organisations.

Why GD?

A group discussion provides a quick way to assess and reject multiple candidates at once. Group discussions don't require any prior preparation, unlike the time consuming tasks involved in written exams like setting question papers and editing countless scripts. The only task left to complete is choosing a topic. However, the candidates are very often given free reign to choose the topic! It is also simple to choose any desired number of candidates, whether it be 4 out of 40 or 2 out of 20. Thus, group discussion is found to be a time- and money-saving technique.

Above all, using group discussion to find a natural leader is the best method. Someone who will emerge as a leader naturally does so in a chaotic setting. This is evident in any student or employee strike. When the strike first starts, there are only a few people who come together for a common cause, but as it goes on, the natural leaders emerge from a large group of followers. These people are all-around good leaders who have excellent coordination skills. Typical management GDs resemble a fish market, where the real leader bargains, settles disputes, coordinates, and works together to make everyone in the group happy.

Employers use group discussion, as an interactive selection process, to evaluate potential candidates' personality traits. A group discussion involves interactive communication among individuals who are connected by a predetermined or chosen topic. Typically, the candidates will have 15 to 20 minutes to respond to the topic. Time is thus a crucial factor in group discussion. Everyone could talk for as long as there was time, on any subject. But when there is a limited amount of time, it requires one to be mentally alert, present, and able to use knowledge within that time. Employers look for a variety of traits when choosing candidates, including: leadership abilities, group management/teamwork skills, communication abilities, reasoning ability, analytical ability, logical and coherent thinking, adaptability and flexibility, positive mental outlook, decent and professional dressing/grooming sense, assertive body language, and projection of a distinctively likable personality.

WHAT IS GROUP DISCUSSION?

Through active and intense interaction, group discussion elicits the opinions of all participants and develops a consensus. Often, introverted people reserve the best opinions for themselves; a sensitive leader among the participants will not only observe this but also gently persuade them to come out. In general, the goal of group discussions is to elicit opinions from everyone involved before reaching an agreement. The final stage of the process that includes conflict, agreement, disagreement, negotiation, and reconciliation is consensus. This is accomplished through a very involved and intense process.

Recognize that the focus of group discussion is GROUP discussion, NOT INDIVIDUAL discussion! As a result, a person cannot select a discussion partner in a group discussion who is a known friend or someone they enjoy speaking with. In fact, group discussions test a person's ability to step outside of their comfort zone, engage in conversation with strangers, and persuade them of something with reason and logic. Because of this, a timid candidate who avoids conversation and only murmurs is disqualified right away in the first round. A candidate should never ignore the fact that there are other participants who are equally interested in sharing their opinions.

Recognize that this is a group discussion, NOT a debate, interview, or public speaking. Discussion refers to a large group of people interacting with one another. When a speaker is in front of a crowd, the audience evaluates him without challenging him. In group discussions, judges are present to rate the participants with whom the other participants are equally competitive. In public speaking, the audience has already granted the speaker leadership. In a group discussion, every candidate has to compete with others to prove himself to be the leader of the group. The judges are looking for leaders in group discussions.

There are two sets of participants in a debate who represent the two opposing sides. There are arguments for and against the motion, as well as points and arguments against them. One group of people is arguing in favour of the motion. The moderator or chairperson is crucial because they preside over the discussion and give it structure. There won't be a moderator to guide the participants of the group discussion to amicably reach a consensus. An interview is a meeting where a panel assesses a candidate's qualifications for the open position. Along with evaluating the candidate's subject knowledge, the panel will also assess their psychological outlook and disposition. However, in the GD, the candidate does not sit alone; rather, they are grouped together with many other people. Additionally, there isn't a visible panel that evaluates candidates by interrogating them. If a panel is used at all to evaluate GD candidates, it will be concealed behind opaque walls. Participants in the group discussion won't see any panels at all.

You will acquire the necessary skills once you have a clear understanding of how group discussion differs from all other speech activities.

There is no moderator, no panel, and no timekeeper during a group discussion, making it an unstructured activity. It is purposefully designed so that a spontaneous structure should develop in tandem with one's capacity to organise an unstructured activity.

The fact that group discussions begin with a group without a leader is another intriguing aspect of them. Nobody is given the responsibility of serving as a leader or moderator. However, those who have assimilated these traits are the ones who will ultimately be chosen from GDs. Since all candidates are rivals and are expected to demonstrate leadership abilities in some way, there is no one leader designated to play the role of moderator in a GD. Without the examiner's presence or involvement, each candidate is expected to participate in the conversation.

A GD can last 15 to 30 minutes and include 10 to 50 participants. One is expected to participate as much as possible within the time allotted while also making sure that everyone's voice is heard.

Components of a GD

Personality manifestation, knowledge, leadership, communication abilities, and are the four fundamental elements of a GD. Initiative, decision-making, planning, and vision are all qualities of a leader. Knowledge implies in-depth subject knowledge, staying current on news and technological developments. Active listening, fluency, clarity, coherence, diction, enunciation, and effectiveness are all aspects of communication skills. Finally, soft skills, body language, a positive outlook, and charming mannerisms can all be used to interpret personality manifestation.

Evaluation Criteria:

Personality	Knowledge	Leadership	Communication Skills
Body language/Gesture	Range	Conflict-resolution skill	Fluency
Dress/Appearance	Logical thinking	Decision-making	Enunciation
Temperament/Tone & V	Depth	Team-spirit/Harmonizir	Diction
Mental state	Organization of ideas	Initiative	Active listening
Over-all impression	Over-all impression	Over-all impression	Over-all impression

Positive traits:

- Personality: Enthusiasm, cheerfulness, keenness, curiosity, smartness, participation.
- Knowledge: Depth, range, organization of ideas, analytical ability, coordination of thoughts.
- Leadership: Team spirit, initiative, decision-making, flexibility, conflict-resolution skills, patience.
- Communication skills: Clarity, felicity of expression, coherence of ideas, categorical conclusion, effectiveness.

Negative traits:

- Personality: Impoliteness, apathy, boredom, lack of confidence, apprehensive.
- Knowledge: Lack of creative ideas, lack of meticulousness, lack of analytical thinking, lack of subject knowledge.
- Leadership: Unapproachable, egoistic, aggressive, isolated, weak and wavering, impatient.
- Communication skills: Meandering, fumbling, confused and unclear, monotony, incoherence.

Leading Group Discussions:

You can either be a discussion igniter or a discussion killer when it comes to guiding group discussion. It goes without saying that you should practice being a conversation starter to ensure your selection. You must be familiar with the words that can be used to start or end a conversation in order to train yourself.

Discussion killers:

- You're wrong
- That's not practical
- That's crazy
- That will never work
- You don't know what you are talking about
- That's ridiculous
- Let's get back to....
- Let's not talk about that

Discussion igniters:

- I agree
- That's a great idea
- That's good
- I'm glad you brought that up
- Really great, anyone else?
- You're on the right track
- I invite other people to join the discussion
- We can do a lot with that idea

Ensuring Success in GDs:

Now let's take a closer look at a few intriguing points that will undoubtedly guarantee success in GDs. You will be ensuring your success in GDs if you observe these norms, adhere to them as serious rules, remember to use them in GDs, repeat them, and keep reviewing them.

- Be assertive (not aggressive)
- Initiate and facilitate discussion
- Be an active listener
- Interfere assertively and politely when the situation demands
- Accept criticism
- Avoid seeking attention
- Be factually and figuratively correct
- Use parliamentary language
- Respect other speakers
- Avoid individual conversations
- Maintain eye contact
- Be precise
- Maximize participation (speak at least 5–6 times)
- Show leadership qualities
- Harmonize
- Control negative body language
- Smile, and speak confidently

Some sample topics:

- Euthanasia: Is it morally right for society?
- Capital punishment- should it be abolished in India
- Relevance of Gandhism today
- Should doctors be tried in Consumer Courts
- Indian bureaucracy- foundation strengths or colonial hangovers?
- Do we need a cut in the defence budget?

- Artificial intelligence- Will man be ever replaced by machines?
- Materialism- Have we sold our souls to the devil?
- Are we unfit for Democracy?
- Should gambling be legalised in India?
- Does India need a dictator?
- Is India moving away from a secularist state?
- Is philosophy just an armchair theory?
- Borderless worlds: Dream or reality?
- Do we need a global policeman?
- If there were no armies in the world....
- We don't learn from history, we repeat it.
- Should people invest in cryptocurrency?
- Urbanization: challenges and remedies
- Brain drain in the Indian context
- Formal degrees are things of the past
- Lessons from the COVID-19 pandemic
- Is technology making us less human?
- Are corporate jobs a new form of slavery?

Practical tips:

- Maintain eye contact throughout the GD.
- Do not look at the judges or evaluators during the GD.
- Sit formally (hands on the thighs, straight back, upright shoulders).
- Use assertive body language to convey active participation (like nodding your head in agreement).
- Motivate the passive team members to contribute to the GD.
- Be progressive, not digressive.

Interview skills:

What is an interview? Why an interview?

Interviews are a formal consultation usually done to evaluate an individual's personality, which cannot be assessed through a written exam. It is interesting to observe the number of personality traits that can be assessed through a personal interview within a matter of 15–20 minutes. For this reason being sufficient enough, almost all the recruiters use personal interviews as one of the methods for recruitment. The interviewer looks for whether the candidate can perform the job in a particular organization and whether they have all the skills to be assigned the responsibility. Personal interviews help employers assess the performance and future potential of a candidate.

Preparation for an interview:

The applicant needs to be ready for the interview mentally, psychologically, and physically. At an interview, the candidate's entire personality is evaluated in addition to his or her knowledge and skills.

Mental Preparation:

- It's important for people looking for work to review the material they studied for exams and courses they have already passed. Up-to-date knowledge in the area of specialisation is required. It is imperative to look over the bio and be prepared to provide more details about all of the listed items, including hobbies and other interests.

- The interview will cover current affairs, significant global and national issues, and important current events. Candidates must be able to discuss current events intelligently and back up their opinions with well-reasoned arguments. Candidates must regularly read newspapers, watch TV news, and participate in current issue discussions.

- The company's annual report contains details about the interviewing company, its owners/directors, its products, its turnover, share capital, organisational structure, when it was published, the locations of the corporate office and branches, growth statistics, development plans, etc. The applicant must learn as much as possible about the organisation whose employment s/he is interested in.

- During an interview, a number of general and biographical questions are posed. Answers to these important questions from a candidate should be succinct and clear, and they should include examples to show their knowledge and abilities.

Psychological Preparation:

Several circumstances or questions during an interview may make the candidate uncomfortable or embarrassed. It is better to plan ahead and have these situations or inquiries ready to go. To handle a depressing circumstance, one needs mental equilibrium. It is necessary to gradually and methodically build up psychological readiness so as to tackle such situations. It is a component of how one develops their personality and character while in school.

- The best course of action when responding to inquiries is candour (being honest). Dishonesty frequently manifests and leaves a negative impression. Admitting that you cannot answer a question is preferable to pretending and speculating. Nobody is expected to be an expert in everything, so it's crucial to understand where information comes from. Being able to admit ignorance of a subject without looking foolish is a plus.
- Lack of discussion skills conveys a negative impression. It is helpful to read up on information about any subject that you find embarrassing to discuss and to practice speaking about it with a few friends. The only way to overcome inhibitions is to confront them.
- At the interview, the subject of pay must be covered. It's crucial to discuss the compensation package without coming off as driven, dejected, or bargaining. An applicant should feel confident negotiating the compensation package if they have knowledge of the salaries offered

for similar jobs, are aware of their qualifications, and have conducted a thorough self-evaluation.

- A candidate must be focused on their goals and steadfast in their desire to learn about their employment prospects. Before leaving, it is necessary to obtain information regarding the nature of the duties, the future outlook, additional benefits, and any other desired information. Making a decision requires the information, especially if there are competing job offers.

Physical Preparation:

- The candidate must present a professional image and wear appropriate attire. Personal hygiene in general, including neatly combed hair and clean, well-trimmed nails, is crucial. The usual standards of formal attire include clean, well-fitting clothing, clean shoes, and a suitable handbag or briefcase.
- Carriage and bearing, or posture, are traits that develop over time and cannot be quickly altered. A candidate's posture and mannerisms while standing, moving, and sitting say a lot about who they are. The candidate's posture and bearing can indicate self-confidence, nervousness, or overconfidence. Keep track of your movements, and be sure to stop any bad habits.
- Good manners and conduct are necessary. The candidate must know what is the appropriate greeting for the time of the day.

What are employers looking for?

- Professionalism

- Self-confidence

- Adaptability/Flexibility

- Motivation

- Good communication skills

- Leadership

- Meticulousness

- Organizational skills

- Ability to work in teams

- Diplomacy

LEADERSHIP OR INITIATIVE

Your employers are primarily interested in your leadership qualities, particularly your capacity for initiative. They want to know if you are a self-starter—someone who works hard because they are driven to do so. They will evaluate both your suitability for the job at hand and your potential for advancement. Prepare yourself to respond to the following inquiries in this context:

What sort of after-school activities have you participated in?

Employers are interested to learn about your extracurricular activities because they will reveal a lot about your leadership abilities. They would learn about your ability to raise money by impressing sponsors, inspiring others to work with you, and your planning skills if you put together a significant event. Your administrative personality will be revealed even if you have only planned minor events like leading quizzes or coordinating a local group discussion programme.

Describe two or three accomplishments of which you are particularly proud of. Explain why you are so proud of them?

Depending on the individuals and the tasks they carry out, different individuals will have different answers to these questions. The answers, however, will reveal one's work ethics, dedication, and level of responsibility. For instance, successfully running a significant event without the actual in-charge (due to an illness or accident) will demonstrate one's capacity to handle the pressure.

MOTIVATION AND GOALS

In addition to your leadership abilities, your employers are interested in your motivations and objectives, which are visible in your research and development activities. Based on your research and development plan, you ought to have established attainable career goals. You should be able to explain these objectives in the context of the company for which you are being interviewed, if necessary. You might be questioned in this context about things like:

Where do you see yourself in the next five years?

You ought to have considered your life goals and created an action plan for the subsequent 25 years before responding to this. To get to where you want to be after 10 years, and so on, you should know what and where you will be in the next 5 years. It doesn't matter if you can reach your goal within the given time frame; what matters is whether you have a clear sense of where you're going. Only when you know where you want to go can you develop focus and dedication.

What made you choose your major?

You cannot claim that you chose your majors because you knew they would lead to lucrative job offers, despite the high salability of these subjects. Employers prioritise finding candidates who are passionate about their chosen fields because they know they will be well-versed in them. In addition, if you are passionate about your subject, you will naturally connect it to your personal objectives and ambitions.

Tell me about yourself.

This is a prime opportunity to make a good impression right away. Don't stutter when you say your name; instead, say it clearly before moving on to other details. You should be able to connect your main objectives and goals to the position you are interviewing for after introducing yourself, briefly outlining your background and CV, and stating your name. You should also include a personality trait that sums up who you are rather well in a single sentence, such as "I try to look for opportunities even in difficult situations." However, if you are asked to give a compelling example to support such a claim, you should be prepared to do so.

Why are you applying for this job?

Saying that you applied for this job because of the high pay package is a silly and immature response to this question. You must claim that the reason is more due to the better career opportunities the job can provide than the financial outlook. You could also claim that you enjoy challenges and that the increased responsibility that the job entails will appeal to you.

What do you know about this job or company?

Another excellent chance to win over your employer. By now, you ought to have enough knowledge about the business to discuss it. Your knowledge of them will give the impression that you have already become a vital part of the business and that choosing you is obvious and essential, regardless of the employer's CV, product line, current issue, competing product, or rival company.

What are your major strengths?

Whether you like it or not, you must list five of your strengths and weaknesses in the format of a brief resume that is now required before attending an interview. Don't, however, fill the format at random with traits that are not unique to you. Additionally, you shouldn't inquire about your strengths from your teachers or friends. Employers are interested in your strengths as well as whether you truly understand them. In your interview, they will question you more about these, so be ready to highlight them with real-world examples.

What is your greatest weakness?

A visionary leader is aware of both his strengths and weaknesses. He is aware of the elements that will contribute to his success and the barriers that will prevent it. Employers are interested in knowing your limitations for this reason. There is nothing to be afraid of, though, because you can honestly list your limitations and determine which one is the biggest weakness. You can discuss why it is the most challenging and the steps you've taken to overcome it in the interview.

Intriguingly, if you look closely, you'll see that sometimes our flaws are also our strengths. For instance, your commitment to perfection might be your best quality. However, that might cause you to succumb to your worst vice, procrastination. Therefore, you can identify procrastination as your greatest weakness while also explaining how your perfectionist attitude is delaying the completion of your work. Another example could be your approach of saying yes to everything that has been put forth, which in fact is taken as a positive trait. This can also prove to be one of your weaknesses, as it can sometimes be overburdening for you. Additionally, it will make a good impression if you can mention some of the constructive measures you have been taking to get around your limitations.

What accomplishment gave you the greatest satisfaction?

The success can be in the workplace, outside of it, or even personally. It should show that you are capable of taking on challenging activities and proving to yourself that you are capable of finishing them (such as learning a foreign language, creating software, or quitting a bad habit).

What are your interests outside of work?

It's an excellent opportunity to discuss your interests and extracurricular activities. Sharing it will undoubtedly earn you some extra credit if you participate in social service and support volunteer groups that help save wildlife, plant trees, donate blood, etc.

What type of work do you like to do best?

Be honest with the interviewers once more and describe the types of work that you enjoy doing without constantly checking your watch.

How do your qualifications or prior experience apply to this position?

If you have changed your career path, you should be able to explain why while looking for ways to apply the knowledge you learned through education to the task at hand.

In what position do you see yourself in five years?

As previously mentioned, the purpose of the question is for the employers to check your goals and make sure they are compatible with those of the business.

What significant issue have you recently resolved?

You cannot claim to have never experienced difficulties. It would be preferable if you could single out one professional or technical challenge you overcame and explain how you did it. Even describing how you quickly made alternative arrangements for a large party that was planned outdoors but ruined by unexpectedly heavy rain will highlight your attention to detail and organisational abilities.

Are you good at handling conflict?

Have you ever fought with a boss or teacher? How did you solve the issue? You won't be rewarded for saying that you are a wonderful person and that you have never argued with your boss or professor. But you will get some credit if you can show that you had a disagreement with your professor or senior and that you handled it wisely.

What are your life objectives? How do you intend to carry out those objectives?

Your career goals and life goals should, in theory, complement one another. Therefore, one of the first steps to achieving those goals should be doing well in the interview and accepting the position. If you are able to provide a detailed plan for achieving those objectives, you will gain credibility.

What would one of your professors say about you if I asked them to sum you up?

Consider at least one professor who values your abilities, knowledge, and goals. S/he should be able to attest to your diligence, perseverance, commitment, dedication, sincerity, reliability, and other qualities.

Which courses did you enjoy the most? Why?

Your favourite classes will reveal a lot about you as well. In contrast to the majority of technological students, who tend to treat people like machines, if you are an engineering student and psychology is your favourite subject, it demonstrates your interest in understanding the human mind.

Why is your GPA/Marks not higher?

This is a tricky question. You need to justify by giving valid reasons. It is interesting to observe though, that no reason is good enough to justify your underperformance. For instance, many people choose to cite that because of their illness, they couldn't score higher. The impression that this leaves on the interviewers is that you let your work and responsibilities suffer for some reason or another, no matter how genuine your reason may be. The best approach to this question is to honestly accept and simply showcase that you've changed. Talk about the things that you did to change this. Convince the interviewers that now you don't let anything hamper your primary duties or responsibilities by also eliciting a few examples.

Would you be open to traveling?

Here, it's crucial that you provide a sincere response. Giving the wrong answer under the impression that you are pleasing the interviewer will only place you in risky situations that you will come to regret. Some people are naturally inclined to enjoy travel and will not object if their job requires any amount of travel. But you should be honest with them if you develop an allergy while traveling that causes you to throw up. The employer can then consider putting you in a profession that doesn't require travel.

How important is money to you? What sort of pay are you seeking?

These are tricky inquiries, so you must respond subtly. You should make it very clear that although money is important in life, it is not everything. Your greedy and overly ambitious nature may be revealed by your demand for an outrageous salary.

Expect the unexpected!

For an interview, one can spend a lifetime preparing. Nevertheless, the part of an interview that is most intriguing, difficult, threatening, humorous, and rewarding is when the candidate is taken off guard by unforeseen questions. However, how one responds to unexpected questions will highlight their creativity and spontaneity. Funny questions are used to gauge a person's capacity for problem-solving under pressure, mental flexibility, good humour, quick thinking, and spontaneity. It aids in eliminating candidates who lack imagination or lateral, unconventional thinking.

Funny questions

- If you were an animal, which animal would you choose to be and why? (also "bird," "tree," "building," "architect," etc.)
- If you were to die tomorrow, what would you do today?

- Sell this pen to me.

- Sell this eraser to me.

- Sell this coconut to me.

- How would you convince an Eskimo to buy a refrigerator?

Preparing questions of your own:

• Will this job involve traveling?

• Does the company provide any training or other educational opportunities for staff?

• What are the avenues for promotion?

• May I see a copy of the job description?

• Why has this job become available?

• Why did the person who held this position leave?

• What qualities are you seeking in a person for this job?

• What would a normal working day be like?

• Can you explain the position and the type of candidate you would like to hire?

• What do you expect from the successful candidate in the first two months?

• How often are performance reviews given?

• Is this a newly created position? If not, what happened to the person who held this position

• Who will the new employee report to?

• Do you see any major changes within the company that will affect this position?

• Is it possible to tour the facility?

• What is the dress code?

• What is the next step?

Structure of an Interview:

- Greeting, receiving, and introducing
- Casual, informal talk to develop rapport
- Formal presentation of your CV by yourself or a panel
- Clarifications on educational background, professional experience, etc.
- Motives for applying for the present job
- Reasons for leaving the previous job
- Assessing suitability for the job
- Acceptability to company's norms and conditions
- Candidate's chance to ask questions
- Thanks, bye, and post-interview operations

What do interviewers like?

- Enthusiasm and energy, not over-ambition

- Modesty, not shyness

- Short, precise answers; not long, convoluted, or meandering

- Self-confidence, not arrogance

- Assertiveness not aggressiveness

What do interviewers dislike?

- Wasting their time
- Repetition
- Over talking
- Unclear explanations
- Too much information
- Aggressive approach
- False interest

After the interview:

Let's discuss what to do after the interview once you've given it your best effort. First, you must follow up with a letter within 48 hours of the interview, especially if the organization's protocol requires it.

You can thank the person for giving you the opportunity to interview. This is the time to send pertinent copies and documents if you said you would send them any missing information.

Additionally, you ought to evaluate your performance and work to improve any weak points. Always keep in mind that no candidate has ever completed an interview by satisfactorily responding to every query. There is always something you feel you should have said or answered better, and you could have generally come across as more confident. Ironically, as soon as you leave the interview location, answers to questions you were unable to address during the interview come to mind.

Even though you gave your best performance and there is a good chance that you will be chosen for the interview, you should use this opportunity to apply for other positions. The more jobs you apply for, the more optimistic you become, which lessens any disappointment you may feel after an interview.

Verbal Aptitude for Employment

Vocabulary Building

Root Words (Etymology)

Words with root and stems are the words that have ' root', generally from Latin/Greek words.

Root could be anything like "EGO" which means "" and can be used in different words like: Egoist or

Egotist. Few more examples of root words:

Amorous, Audible, Autocracy, Benefactor, Decapitate, Chronology, Bibliography

Collocations

Collocation Is a familiar group of words which appears together because of their habitual use and thus creating the same meaning.

Verb Collocation

-To save time

-You will save a lot of time if you concentrate on your studies rather than browsing the net.

Adjective Collocation

- Deep feeling, deep sleep, deep trouble

- Heavy rain, heavy traffic, heavy snow

- Strong smell, strong denial

Noun Collocation

Service industry, tea leaf, blurred vision, hard-earned money

Prefixes and Suffixes

Addition of some letter/s in the beginning of any word is called a prefix and if the same addition is done at the end of the word, it is called a suffix.

Examples of Prefix

Uncomfortable, Amoral, Supernatural, Autobiography, Foretell, Misfortune, Vice-President, Tricolour, Cooperate

Examples of Suffix

Childhood, Booklet, Organization, Amazement, Popularize, Beautifully, Lengthwise, Exploration, Happiness

Standard Abbreviations

Abbreviations are condensed versions of long words or phrases. They are prevalent across almost all fields of study and spheres of life. For example, commonly used abbreviations in names or titles, such as MR. for mister, Pres. for president, and DR. for doctor.

An acronym is a new word created from the initial letters of a long name or phrase.

For Example

NATO: Northern Atlantic Treaty Organization

FBI: Federal Bureau of Investigation

Common Abbreviations

Approx: Approximately

Appt : Appointment

ASAP: As soon as possible

DIY: Do it yourself

Synonyms and Antonyms

-An effective use of synonyms and antonyms is essential to both written and oral communication. The English language's vocabulary must be understood in order to express oneself effectively. A word's semantic relationship or synonym refers to a word's similar meaning.

A word or phrase that has the same meaning as another word or phrase in the same language is said to have a lexical similarity. The negative connotation of a word is what makes it an antonym.

-An antonym is a word or phrase that has the exact opposite meaning to another word or phrase of the same language.

Some examples of synonyms of a word and its antonym put in the bracket.

1. Kindred: Relation, species (unrelated, dissimilar)

2. Keen : Sharp, poignant (vapid, insipid)

3. Knave: Dishonest, scoundrel (paragon, innocent)

4. Knell: Death knell, last blow (reconstruction, rediscovery)

5. Knotty: Complicated difficult (simple, manageable)

6. Luxuriant: Profuse, abundant (scanty, meager)

7. Luscious: Palatable, delicious (unsavoury, tart)

8. Lure: Attract, entice (repel, dissuade)

9. Lunacy: Delusion, insanity (normalcy, sanity)

10. Lucid: Sound, rational (obscure, hidden)

11. Listless: Indifferent, inattentive (brisk, attentive)

12. Linger: loiter, prolong (hasten, quicken)

13. Liberal: Magnanimous, generous (stingy, malicious)

14. Liable: Accountable, bound (unaccountable, apt to)

15. Lenient: Compassionate, merciful (cruel, severe)

16. Lax: Slack, careless (firm, reliable)

17. Lavish: Abundant, excessive (scarce, deficient)

18. Mutual : Joint, identical (separate, distinct)

19. Mutinous: Recalcitrant, insurgent (submissive, faithful)

20. Murky: Dusky, dreary (bright shining)

21. Munificent : Liberal, hospitable (frugal, penurious)

22. Monotonous: Irksome, tedious (varied, pleasant)

23. Momentous: Notable, eventful (trivial, insignificant)

24. Mollify : Appease, assuage (irritate, infuriate)

25. Molest: Harass, tease (console, soothe)

26. Modest : Humble, courteous (arrogant, pompous)

27. Mitigate: Alleviate, relieve (augment, enhance)

28. Miraculous: Marvelous, extraordinary (ordinary, trivial)

29. Minute : Diminutive, miniature (large, colossal)

30. Numerous: Profuse, various (scarce, deficient)

31. Nullify : Cancel, annual (confirm, uphold)

32. Noxious : Baneful, injurious (healing, profitable)

33. Novice : Tyro, beginner (veteran, ingenious)

34. Nonchalant : Indifferent, negligent (attentive, considerate)

35. Nimble : Prompt, brisk (sluggish, languid)

36. Niggardly : Miser, covetous (generous, profuse)

37. Negligent : Inattentive, careless (vigilant, careful)

38. Overwhelm : Triumph, subjugate (flounder, falter)

39. Outrage : Offense, maltreatment (praise, favour)

40. Outbreak: Eruption, insurrection (compliance, subjection)

41. Ornamental: Decorative, adorned (unseemly, plain)

42. Ordain: Order, impose (revoke, abolish)

43. Oracular : Cryptic, vague (lucid, distinct)

44. Opaque: Obscure, shady (transparent, bright)

45. Offspring: Descendant, sibling (ancestor, forefather)

46. Offensive: Abhorrent, arrogant (docile, compliant)

47. Odious: Malevolent, obnoxious (engaging, fascinating)

48. Occult: latent, ambiguous (intelligible, transparent)

49. Obvious: Evident, apparent (obscure, ambiguous)

50. Obstruct: Impede, prevent (hasten, encourage)

51. Prudent: Cautious, discreet (impetuous, unwise)

52. Provoke: Inflame, incite (pacify, comfort)

53. Protract : Prolong, delay (abbreviate, curtail)

54. Proscribe: Prohibit, exclude (solicit, include)

55. Profuse: Lavish, abundant (scarce, scantly)

56. Profligate: Dissolute, degenerate (virtuous, upright)

57. Prodigy : Miracle, marvel (normal, average)

58. Prodigious: Vast, enormous (unimpressive, diminutive)

59. Premature: Precocious, untimely (belated, opportune)

60. Predicament: Plight, dilemma (resolution, confidence)

61. Precarious : Doubtful, insecure (assured, undeniable)

62. Pompous: Haughty, arrogant (unpretentious, humble)

63. Perverse: Petulant, obstinate (complacent, docile)

64. Pertness: Flippancy, impudence (modesty, diffidence)

65. Peevish: Perverse, sullen (suave, amiable)

66. Peerless : Matchless, unrivaled (mediocre, commonplace)

67. Paramount : Foremost, eminent (trivial, inferior)

68. Pamper: Flatter, indulge (deny, disparage)

69. Placid: Tranquil, calm (turbulent, hostile)

70. Quell: Subdue, reduce (exacerbate, agitate)

71. Quaint: Queer, strange (familiar, usual)

72. Quack: Impostor, deceiver (upright, unfeigned)

73. Quibble: Equivocate, prevaricate (unfeign, plain)

74. Quarantine: Seclude, screen (befriend, socialize)

75. Questionable : Dubious, disputable (reliable, authentic)

76. Reverence: Respect, esteem (disrespect, affront)

77. Ratify: Consent, approve (deny, dissent)

78. Ravage: Destroy, ruin (reconstruct, renovate)

79. Redeem: Recover, liberate (conserve, lose)

80. Ruthless: Remorseless, inhumane (compassionate, lenient)

81. Rustic: Rural uncivilised (cultured, refined)

82. Rout: Vanquish, overthrow (succumb, withdraw)

83. Retract : Recant, withdraw (confirm, assert)

84. Remote: Inaccessible, farther (adjoining, adjacent)

85. Remorse: Regret, penitence (ruthlessness, obduracy)

86. Resentment: Displeasure, wrath (content, cheer)

87. Rescind : Annul, abrogate (delegate, permit)

88. Remonstrate: Censure, protest (agree, laud)

89. Remnant: Residue, piece (entire, whole)

90. Sycophant: Parasite, flatterer (devoted, loyal)

91. Superficial: Partial, shallow (profound, discerning)

92. Subvert: Demolish, sabotage (generate, organise)

93. Substantial: Considerable, solid (tenuous, fragile)

94. Subsequent: Consequent, following (Preceding, Previous)

95. Stain: Blemish, tarnish (honour, purify)

96. Scanty: Scarce, insufficient (lavish, multitude)

97. Sarcastic: Ironical, derisive (courteous, gracious)

98. Shrewd: Cunning, crafty (simple, imbecile)

99. Stupor: Lethargy, unconsciousness (sensibility, consciousness)

100. Squalid: Dirty, filthy (tidy, attractive)

101. Sporadic: Intermittent, scattered (incessant, frequent)

102. Solicit: Entreat, implore (protest, oppose)

103. Sneer: Mock, scorn (flatter, praise)

104. Slander: Defame, malign (applaud, approve)

105. Shabby: Miserable, impoverished (prosperous, thriving)

106. Saucy: Impudent, insolent (modest, humble)

107. Tyro: Beginner, learner (proficient, veteran)

108. Trivial: Trifling, insignificant (significant veteran)

109. Trenchant: Assertive, forceful (feeble, ambiguous)

110. Transient: Temporal, transitory (lasting, enduring)

111. Tranquil: Peaceful, composed (violent, furious)

112. Timid: Diffident, coward (bold, intrepid)

113. Temperate: Cool, moderate (boisterous, violent)

114. Tedious: Wearisome, irksome (exhilarating, lively)

115. Taciturn: Reserved, silent (talkative, extrovert)

116. Taboo: Prohibit, ban (permit, consent)

117. Throng: Assembly, crowd (dispersion, sparsity)

118. Tumultuous: Violent, riotous (peaceful, harmonious)

119. Utterly: Completely, entirely (deficiently, incompletely

120. Usurp: Seize, wrest (restore, compensate)

121. Uncouth: Awkward, ungraceful (elegant, graceful)

122. Umbrage : Resentment, bitterness (sympathy, goodwill)

123. Vulgar: Inelegant, offensive (elegant, civil)

124. Vouch: Confirm, consent (repudiate, prohibit)

125. Volatile: light, changing (heavy, ponderous)

126. Vicious: Corrupt, obnoxious (noble, virtuous)

127. Venerable: Esteemed, honoured (unworthy, immature)

128. Vanity: Conceit, pretension (modesty, humility)

129. Valour: Bravery, prowess (fear, cowardice)

130. Vagrant: Wanderer, roaming (steady, settled)

131. Viellant : Cautious, alert (careless, negligent)

132. Valid: Genuine, authentic (fallacious, deceptive)

133. Veteran: Ingenious, experienced (novice, tyro)

134. Venom : Poison, malevolence (antidote, benevolent)

135. Waive: Relinquish, remove (impose, clamp)

136. Wary: Cautious, circumspect (heedless, negligent)

137. Wane: Decline, dwindle (ameliorate, rise)

138. Wilt: Wither, perish (revive, bloom)

139. Wield: Use, employ (forgo, avoid)

140. Wan: Pale, faded (bright, healthy)

141. Wicked: Vicious, immoral (virtuous, noble)

142. Wed: Marry, combine (divorce, separate)

143. Yoke: Connect, harness (liberate, release)

144. Yield: Surrender, abdicate (resist, protest)

145. Yearn: Languish, crave (content, satisfy)

146. Yell: Shout, shriek (whisper, muted)

147. Zest: Delight, enthusiasm (disgust, passive)

148. Zenith : Summit, apex (nadir, base)

149. Zeal: Eagerness, fervour (apathy, lethargy)

150. Zig-zag: Oblique, wayward (straight, unbent)

A few one word substitution:

1. Audience: A number of people listening to a lecture.

2. Altruist: One, who considers the happiness and well-being of others first.

3. Atheist: A person who does not believe in God.

4. Anthropologist: One, who studies the evolution of mankind

5. Autocracy: Government by one person.

6. Autobiography: The life history of a person written by himself

7. Amputate: To cut off a part of a person's body which is infected

8. Arsenal: a place for ammunition and weapons

9. Archives : A place where government or public records are kept

10. Amateur: A man who does a thing for pleasure and not as a profession

11. Aristocracy: Government by the nobles

12. Aquatic: Animals/plants which live in water

13. Amphibian : Animals which live both on land and sea

14. Ambidexter : One, who can use either hand with ease

15. Alimony: Allowance paid to wife on legal separation

16. Anthology: A collection of poems

17. Abdication: Voluntary giving up of throne in favour of someone

18. Arbitrator: A person, appointed by two parties to solve a dispute

19. Astronomer: A person, who studies stars, planets and other heavenly bodies

20. Astrologer: A person who studies the influence of heavenly bodies on human beings

21. Anthology: A collection of poems

22. Axiom: A statement which is accepted as true without proof

23. Agenda: Aa list of headings of the business to be transacted at a meeting

24. Anarchist: One who is out to destroy all governance, law and order

25. Almanac: An annual calendar with positions of stars

26. Bigamy: The practice of having two wives or husbands at a time

27. Bibliophile: A lover and collector of books

28. Bouquet: A collection of flowers

29. Bureaucracy: Government by the officials

30. Belligerent: A person, nation that is involved in war

31. Biennial: An event which happens once in two years

32. Blasphemy: The act of speaking disrespectfully about sacred things

33. Crèche: A nursery where children are cared for while their parents are at work

34. Cosmopolitan: A person who regards whole world as his country

35. Chauffeur: One who is employed to drive a motor car

36. Curator: A person in charge of a museum

37. Carnivorous: One who lives on flesh,

38. Cannibal : One who feeds on human flesh

39. Contemporaries: Belonging to or living at the same time

40. Cloak room : A place for luggage at railway station

41. Cynosure: Centre of attraction

42. Connoisseur: A critical judge of any art and craft

43. Crusade: A religious war

44. Choreographer: One who teaches dancing

45. Cacographist : A person, who is bad in spellings

46. Calligraphist: A person, who writes beautiful handwriting

47. Cynic: One who sneers at the aims and beliefs of his fellow men

48. Convalescent: One who is recovering health

49. Cavalry: Soldiers, who fight on horseback

50. Cardiologist: A person, who is specialist in heart diseases

51. Cartographer: One who draws maps u

52. Dormitory: The sleeping rooms with several beds especially in a college or institution

53. Drawn: A game that results neither in victory nor in defeat

54. Elegy: A poem of lamentation

55. Epitaph: Words which are inscribed on the grave or the tomb in the memory of the buried

56. Ephemeral; Lasting one day

57. Effeminate: A person who is womanish

58. Emigrant: A person who leaves his own country and goes to live in another

59. Edible: Fit to be eaten

60. Egotism: Practice of talking too much about oneself

61. Encyclopaedia: A book that contains information on various subjects

62. Epicure: One, who is devoted to the pleasure of eating and drinking

63. Florist: One who deals-in flowers

64. Fastidious: One who is very -selective in one's taste

65. Fanatic or Bigot: One who is filled with excessive and mistaken enthusiasm in religious matters

66. Fatal: Causing death

67. Fatalist: One who believes in fate

68. Facsimile: An exact copy of handwriting, printing etc.

69. Fauna: The animals of a certain region

70. Flora: The plants of a particular region

71. Fratricide : Murder of brother

72. Fugitive: One who runs away from justice or the law

73. Fragile : Easily broken

74. Feminist : One who works for the welfare of the women g

75. Granary: A place for grains

76. Genocide : Murder of race

77. Gregarious: Animals which live in flocks

78. Hangar: A place for housing airplanes

79. Hive: A place for bees

80. Horticulture: The art of cultivating and managing gardens

81. Homicide : Murder of man

82. Hearse: A vehicle which is used to carry a dead body

83. Hedonist: One who believes that pleasure is the chief good (sensual)

84. Horizon: A line at which the earth and the sky seem to meet

85. Honorary : Holding office without any remuneration

86. Heretic: Ane who acts against religion

87. Herbivorous: One who lives on herbs

88. Insolvent/Bankrupt: A person who is unable to pay his debts

89. Inaudible: A sound that cannot be heard

90. Inaccessible: that cannot be easily approached

91. Incorrigible: incapable of being corrected

92. Irreparable: Incapable of being repaired

93. Illegible: Incapable of being read

94. Inevitable: Incapable of being avoided

95. Impracticable: Incapable of being practise

96. Immigrant: A person who comes to one country from another in order to settle there

97. Invincible: One, too strong to be overcome

98. Indelible: That cannot be erased

99. Incognito: Traveling under another name than one's own

100. Indefatigable: One who does not tire easily

101. Infallible: One who is free from all mistakes and failures

102. Invigilator: One who supervises in the examination hall

103. Itinerant: One who journeys from place to place

104. Infirmary: A home or room used for ill or injured people

105. Infanticide: Murder of an infant

106. Infantry: Soldiers, who fight on foot

107. Inflammable: liable to catch fire easily

108. Interregnum: A period of interval between two reigns or governments

109. Kennel: A place-for dogs

110. Lunatic asylum: A home for lunatics

111. Lexicographer: One who compiles a dictionary

112. Loquacious: One who talks continuously

113. Linguist: One who is skilled in foreign languages

114. Lapidist : One who cuts precious stones

115. Misanthrope: A hater of mankind

116. Misogamist: One who hates marriage

117. Mortuary: A place, where dead bodies are kept for post mortem

118. Mercenary: Working only for the sake of money

119. Matricide: Murder of mother

120. Martyr: One, who dies for a noble cause

121. Maiden speech: The first speech delivered by a person

122. Mint: A place where coins are made

123. Misogynist: A hater of womankind

124. Morgue: A place, where dead bodies are kept for identification

125. Mammals: Animals which give milk

126. Monogamy: The practice of marrying one at a time

127. Missionary: A person, who is sent to propagate religion

128. Numismatics : The study of coins

129. Namesake: A person having same name as another

130. Nostalgia: A strong desire to return. home, home sickness

131. Novice or Tyro: One, new to anything, inexperienced

132. Narcotic: A medicine for producing sleep

133. Optimist: A person who looks at the brighter side of things

134. Orphan: One, who has lost parents

135. Omnipresent : One who is present everywhere

136. Omnipotent: One who is all powerful

137. Omniscient : One who knows everything

138. Opaque: That which cannot be seen through

139. Obituary: An account in the newspaper of the funeral of the one deceased

140. Orphanage: A home for orphans

141. Obstetrician: One who is skilled in midwifery

142. Ostler: One who looks after horses at an inn

143. Omnivorous: One who eats everything

144. Pessimist: A person who looks at the darker side of things

145. Potable: Fit to drink

146. Post mortem: An examination of dead body

147. Philanthropist: A lover of mankind

148. Patricide: Murder of father

149. Philatelist: One who collects stamps

150. Plagiarism: literary theft or passing off an author's original work as one's own

151. Polygamy: The practice of marrying more than one wife at a time

152. Polyandry: The practice of marrying more than one husband at a time

153. Philogynist: A lover of womankind

154. Plebiscite: (A decision made by) votes of all qualified citizens

155. Philanderer: One who amuses himself by love making

156. Philistine: One who does not care for art and literature

157. Plutocracy: Government by the rich

158. Pseudonym: An imaginary name assumed by an author for disguise

159. Posthumous: A child born after the death of his father or the book published after the death of the writer.

160. Panacea: A remedy for all diseases.

161. Pediatrician: A person, who is specialist in child diseases

162. Platitude: Ordinary remarks often repeated

163. Pedant: One who makes a vain display of his knowledge

164. Polyglot : One who speaks many languages

165. Paleography: the study of ancient writing

166. Posse: A number of policemen called to quell a riot

167. Parole: Pledge given by a prisoner for temporary release, not to escape

168. Pedestrian: One who goes on foot

169. Portable: That can be carried easily

170. Quarantine: An act of separation from other persons to avoid infection

171. Rhetoric: The art of elegant speech or writing

172. Regicide: Murder of King or Queen

173. Sacrilege: Violating or profaning religious things/places

174. Sculptor: One who cuts in stones

175. Suicide : Murder of oneself

176. Stable: A place for horses

177. Somnambulist: A person, who walks in sleep

178. Somniloquist : A person, who talks in sleep

179. Souvenir: A thing kept as a reminder of a person, place or event

180. Swan song: The last work (literary) of a writer

181. Sot, Toper: One who is a habitual drunkard

182. Sinecure: A job with high salary but little responsibility

183. Stoic : A person, who is indifferent to pleasure and pain and has control over his passions

184. Sanatorium: A place for the sick to recover health

185. Sororicide: Murder of sister

186. Triennial : An event which happens once in three years

187. Truant: A person/student who absents himself from class or duty without permission

188. Teetotaller: One who does not take any intoxicating drink

189. Transparent: That which can be seen through

190. Theocracy: Government by religious principles

191. Uxorious: One extremely fond of one's wife

192. Utopia: An imaginary perfect social and political system

193. Uxoricide : Murder of wife

194. Verbatim: Repetition of speech or writing word for word

195. Volunteer: One who offers one's services

196. Virgin: A woman who has no sexual experience

197. Versatile: Interested in and clever at many different things

198. Veteran: One who has a long experience of any occupation

199. Venial: A fault that may be forgiven

200. Wardrobe: A place for clothes

Identifying Common Errors:

Following are some common grammatical mistakes people often make :

Wrong: I congratulate you for your success.

Right: I congratulate you on your success.

Wrong: Open on page 120.

Right: Open at page 120.

Wrong: The reception will be held between 5 to 10 p.m.

Right: The reception will be held between 5 and 10 p.m.

Wrong: He is good in English.

Right: He is good at English.

Wrong: The train came in time.

Right: The train came on time.

Wrong: We have no tea nor sugar.

Right: We have no tea or sugar.

Wrong: Write the cheque for five hundred fifty rupees.

Right: Write the cheque for five hundred and fifty rupees.

Wrong: Good night, I am happy to meet you.

Right: Good evening, I am happy to meet you.

Wrong: More sweets? Thank you.

Right: More sweets? No, thank you

Wrong: There is no place for me in the compartment.

Right: There is no room for me in the compartment.

Wrong: The child is learning Alphabets.

Right: The child is learning Alphabet.

Wrong: The ship, with all its crew, were destroyed.

Right: The ship, with all its crew, was destroyed.

Wrong: I bought two dozens mangoes.

Right: I bought two dozen mangoes.

Wrong: I have two brother-in-laws.

Right: I have two brothers-in-law.

Wrong: He hit two boundaries and three sixers.

Right: He hit two fours and three sixes.

Wrong: I need one and a half rupee.

Right: I need one and half rupees.

Wrong: This is Verma's, our professor's house.

Right: This is Verma, our professor's house.

Wrong: He obtained just passing marks.

Right: He obtained just pass marks.

Wrong: Jabalpur is further from Delhi than Agra.

Right: Jabalpur is further from Delhi that it is from Agra

Wrong: The patient died before the doctor came.

Right: The patient had died before the doctor came.

Wrong: Two and two makes four.

Right: Two and two make four.

Wrong: He ran as fast as he can.

Right: He ran as fast as he could.

Wrong: If you will work hard, you will pass.

Right: If you work hard, you will pass.

Wrong: He did nothing but laughed.

Right: He did nothing but laugh.

Wrong: The painting hanged on the wall.

Right: The painting hung on the wall.

Wrong: The boy, as well as the girls, need care.

Right: The boy, as well as the girls, needs care.

Wrong: He behaves as if he is the king.

Right: He behaves as if he was the king.

(As if is followed, by the past tense)

Wrong: Open this knot.

Right: Untie this knot.

Wrong: When shall I give the examination?

Right: When shall I take the examination?

Wrong: My mother who is an artist is unwell.

Right: My mother, who is an artist, is unwell.

(The first sentence means: I have many mothers, and the one who is an artist is not well. The second sentence means: My mother is an artist, and she is unwell. The commas make the difference.)

Wrong: Abdul has a dog to sell who wishes to go abroad.

Right: Abdul, who wishes to go abroad, has a dog to sell.

Wrong: I shall return just now.

Right: I shall return presently.

(just now does not relate to future)

Wrong: I repent for my misdeed.

Right: I repent of my misdeed.

Wrong: The breakfast is ready.

Right: Breakfast is ready.

Wrong: The Prime Minister Nehru was a great writer.

Right: Prime Minister Nehru was a great writer.

Wrong: Rajiv Gandhi, the son of Indira Gandhi, was a popular leader.

Right: Rajiv Gandhi, son of Indira Gandhi, was a popular leader.

Wrong: What kind of a man is he?

Right: What kind of man is he?

Wrong: I have headache.

Right: I have a headache.

Wrong: Give me an inkpot or pen.

Right: Give me an inkpot or a pen.

Wrong: I take your leave.

Right: I take leave of you.

Wrong: One should do his duty well.

Right: One should do one's duty well.

Wrong: I beg your favour of considering me for the post.

Right: I beg the favour of you considering me for the post.

Wrong: She is fairer than him.

Right: She is fairer than he is.

Wrong: It is me.

Right: It is I.

Wrong: His shirt is better than his friend.

Right: His shirt is better than that of his friend.

Wrong: While reading Hamlet, the monkey caught my eye.

Right: While I was reading Hamlet, the monkey caught my eye.

Wrong: When only four, my mother taught me to read.

Right: When I was only four, my mother taught me to read.

Wrong: I am here since two days.

Right: I have been here for two days.

Wrong: He has left for Mumbai yesterday.

Right: He left for Mumbai yesterday.

Printed in Great Britain
by Amazon

42581862R00040